I AIN'T JEALOUS of DEBT!

Breaking the chains that controls, possesses, oppresses, torments, and vexes 4 out of 5 people:

Fear one of the signs of jealousy!

By Cassie Brewer

Published by

Total Victory in Christ Ministries

I Ain't Jealous of debt!

I said Ain't

Because

"Am Not"

Is not Strong

Enough

 Scripture quotations are from the King James Version. (KJV)

TABLE OF CONTENTS

INTRODUCTION

I Ain't Jealous of debt. I know Ain't is not a word that should be used in proper grammar. I tried to use "Am Not," but it was not a strong enough word to tell my readers how defeated I felt.

I was in prison without physical bars. I was walking around in depression. I believe in total victory, and I was not walking in it. I had to conquer my enemy and slay it. So, I could prevent my past spending habits from moving into my future and get to one of the depths of fear that needed to be rooted out.

The information contained in this book is destined to shake you into becoming financially free. We must examine our priorities and our approach in healing. We emphasize the healing of body and soul while the cry for financial freedom is ignored!

This book will help you no longer be plagued with memories of financial failure. It will help stop the bully of overspending. I will encourage you to find the root cause of repeating the same mistake repeatedly.

It will help you face your shortcoming, denial, and fear. It will lead you to the door of escape.

ACKNOWLEDGMENTS

First giving honor to God who is the head of my life. Thank you for the blood shed of Jesus. We can catapult into the spirit realm and access the true power for healing, deliverance, and financial freedom.

May our Lord and Savior be praised forever. My name may appear on the cover. But as a member of the body of Christ. We are members one with another and tied to each other through the Holy spirit.

I wish to acknowledge the following individuals for their contribution to this work. First my husband Anthony the most supportive man in the world, for his partnership in the ministry and lessons we have learned together. Especially the practice lesson in compassion and love.

To my silent partners in ministry: thanks, Brianna West Brewer for continuing to press me into becoming the author of this book and to start a financial freedom class, and for designing the cover of this book, Tameca Brewer Dinkins for your faithfulness and commitment, Dynasty U. Brewer for your encouragement, Anthony Brewer Jr.

for believing in me, Paris Brewer Dumas for all your love, Alvin Dinkins J.R. for your statement God do not play, and Allen Dumas for all your prayers. And to the Total Victory in Christ Ministry, thank you for supporting me, believing in me, and enabling me to give time to the word of God and prayer.

Debt

Have you ever felt like everybody around you was living the life you are working so hard for yourself, but you are struggling just to make ends meet? I felt like that!

I remember years ago, one morning my husband called me while driving to work. I could hear tears in his voice. I asked him, what is wrong; He was a little bit hesitant to respond.

He said I do not understand why God is blessing all these people that is not serving him and the ones that are, is stuck in the struggle. We work in the church, we are at every program to support the ministry and work our gift, we give to the food ministry, we pay tithes; I feel like God is blessing everybody else but his people financially.

It seems as if the more I work, the less there is to spend, but our neighbors got it going on. They can live anyway they want to, and not have to be worried about working a 9-5 job. From the looks of it, they have the best things, and make it look so easy to obtain. I could only think of one scripture to tell him (Ps. 37:1-9).

Do not worry because of evildoers, and do not be envious toward wrongdoers. When I got off the phone, I started to wonder if I had given advice to him that I should use myself? I know more people are wondering too.

God created us to have a relationship with him from the beginning of time. But the disobedience by Adam and Eve brought sin into God's creation and our perfect relationship with Him was shattered. We became separated from God physically, spiritually and I believe financially. Even today we all sin and fall short of His perfect design. But I was determined to be financially free.

Find the truth for yourself

Study to show yourself approved unto God, a workman that needed not be ashamed, rightly dividing the word of truth (2 Tim.2:15). Everybody was not born with a silver spoon in their mouth, nor did they do illegal things to get it either. So, what was my issue?

I know with our salaries these things are not possible to obtain, I thought; We just have to many bills! One morning after doing prayer time. I turn on the radio and heard a man say you got to live like nobody else so you can live like nobody else.

He was living the American dream and lost it. I continued to listen to him, and I thought this is impossible to do. I later found out this man's name was Dave Ramsey. His radio time was 2:30pm.

Something about this broadcast excited me. So, I made time in my busy schedule just to hear him. I started to apply some of the things he was saying on the radio to our life, because I could not afford to take a financial class, plus I knew I would fail at it and waste what little money I had. The first thing was to find the difference between snowball and avalanche. Snowball, you pay your bills from least amount to the highest amount. The avalanche, you pay from the highest to the least amount. Ok, which would work for me?

Then I found out about the envelop stuffing with cash! I knew this was the one for me. I start using the envelops, with cash in them instead of credit cards; paying with the cash money to stay on track with my spending.

Things was going great for us! We were now in control of our finances.

It is time for a celebration, we are on our way to becoming financially free. We had a saving and paid off three credit cards.

Wait for it

We were celebrating our victory. We stayed in victory so long celebrating; we took our eyes off the enemy for a second. It does not take long for the enemy to knock you out of the present back into the past.

The devil comes to kill, steal, and destroy. He killed our mood, stole our peace and was trying to destroy our oneness. While celebrating, there was a knock at the door. Our neighbors came over to show us their new truck and the diamond ring that I have been looking at for so long; she has it.

They came over on the day of our celebration of being debt free; We had mixed emotions. We should have discussed this mixed emotion, but we did not. We acted like it did not happen.

Have you ever pretended something did not bother you when it really did. A month later, our other neighbors got a new house and was leaving the neighborhood. On the same day we paid off another bill.

We were completely without funds, and they were having the time of their lives. My husband said, I know we make more money than them, and we cannot afford a new home. What are we doing wrong? I replied I do not know, but I am tired of sitting around here, eating noodles, hot dogs and paying bills. I miss eating what I want, when I want, where I want! My husband said, let us get out of this house. Yes, we needed to get out of the house and a break from budgeting.

We are completely focusing on getting out of debt and our neighbors were focusing on getting into debt. They were enjoying the fruits of their labor. Have you ever heard; you cannot see the forest for the trees? We could not see that we were on the right track.

Leaving the house was a big mistake! We took our eyes off the prize and did something dumb! We will soon find out; we have an underlining condition when it comes to debt.

The Dumb things we do

Spending hundreds on eating out, vacations and things we did not need or want. Over the next few months, we were back where we started! No money and in credit card debt again; the joke was on us.

We had no one else to blame! We did this to ourselves. How dumb can you be, we thought! We were a shame and embarrassed, plain ignorant. In the words of Forrest Gump, stupid is what stupid does. We had done something stupid again. I could hear Dave Ramsey say, that is just stupid! No one knew we had failed, but us.

We were like Adam and Eve in the garden, naked and afraid. We failed at Budgeting again, we were to shame and proudful, to call out to God for help. We wanted to let Him know, we are in debt again, as if the Lord did not already know.

It is funny how we get into debt without acknowledging God, until it is time to pay up. Now we want to acknowledge God for help to get us out of debt. The nightmare of debt had returned, vigorously. We were throwing money away on things that do not build freedom of life.

We were in more debt now, then we ever were. We had to start all over again! The worry, doubt and unbelief came flooding in. I fell to my knees, and said Lord what is wrong with us? We did it again! Back in debt. Have you ever got out of a situation, and find yourself back in it again?

I do not want to ever attend this type of party again. The party of repeated stupidity! We surrender to the direction of God and was ready for the repercussions, of this mess we created.

Money is just a tool

We are not in control of our finances, as we thought. God said," the love of money, is the root to all evil" it makes people do things that they never thought they would do.

The Apostle Paul wrote, all wrongdoing can be traced to an excessive attachment to material wealth, while some coveted after, they have erred from the faith, and pierced themselves with many sorrows. Meaning, some financial wounds are self-inflicted. We were walking looking like Swiss cheese. The bacteria in debt grow like the gases in Swiss cheese, they emit up creating wounds in your finances.

There are only three things we can do with money, save it, spend it, and give it away. We had the spending and the giving it away down to a science. We were not spending it on real estate or investments, we did not save anything for our future.

Emotional spending does not lead to financial freedom, but it will put you in the poor house! We were well on our way to the poor house. Because our understanding about money, and how it works, was all wrong!

It was wisdom or foolish deadline day. We had to make a choice. We have been foolish for years. It is time for a change! We were ready to receive more from God as to why our spending habits are out of control.

Having money and spending money cannot be the end goal. I begin to meditate and encourage myself to keep discovering the root cause of this revolving debt crisis.

Now that we have the right concept about money. My heart is ready to go deeper in my search for financial freedom. God spoke to me and said,

research the difference between
jealousy and envy.

Be careful what you ask for, you just might get it.

As I begin to study these two words, they both involve feeling of desire for what someone else has. The first thing caught my attention was feelings. We all know feelings change. It is an emotional state or reaction.

The good thing about having feelings is, they change. Now, desire is a different ball game. It means to crave, want or longing for. This means to wish to obtain or a strong want. I knew when I heard jealousy and envy, I was entering into a territory I did not want to go. I begin to tread lightly. Because when you seek the Lord about something.

You better be ready because He is the truth. The Lord loves you and will not sugar coat anything to spare your feeling. He wants what is best for you at any cost. Envy is the emotion of coveting what someone else has. It implies strong envious desire.

The bible calls it lust. Notably for another's possession. The bible has several negative consequences for lusting or coveting after something. Right now, all kind of emotions are running through me. I was praying that God did not tell me to research this for myself.

Now, jealousy is an emotion related to fear. A feeling of unhappiness caused by wanting what someone else has. "I want what you have, and until I have it, you should not have it either. This hit me like a freight train! When I came to myself, my mind was unsettled.

I ran to discuss it with my husband! After I told him the meaning of jealousy, he stood there like a deer in head lights. His response was, we were afraid that we could not obtain the abundant life we wanted at the paste we were traveling and did not want anyone else to have it if we could not.

Be careful what you ask for, you just might get it. I was in complete denial, not me! This could not be the reason we keep getting into debt. Not me, jealous! I love celebrating your accomplishments to get to the American dream, I thought.

Diagnosis

I was sure the Lord had miss diagnosed me! He made a mistake. This was a word for my husband. He received that word from God that day with no hesitation.

He said, Lord I apologize, and went his way. He was walking around praying saying thank you for showing me the error of my ways. He was just humbling himself before the Lord, thank you for another chance to get it right.

I went on for a few days denying it. But every time I passed a mirror, I could hear, your jealous too. I replied not me! God was talking to my husband do not get it twisted. Now this jealous thing is getting to me.

I can hear myself, talking to myself, I thought. I started talking back to the voice that was talking to me so loudly. I shouted, will you be quiet and stop talking to me every time I pass a mirror. Being jealous is not a part of me! This was tormenting me, leave me alone I said.

Early one morning before I got to the mirror, I told the mirror, He was not talking to me before you say to me you are jealous. But this time the voice said, yes, I am talking too you! You have a spirit of jealousy. I pleaded with God to let it be anything but jealousy. What am I so jealous of.

The Lord responded, debt. I know I am not hearing this right, because how can you be jealous of debt? I do not understand, the Lord replied: you are jealous of people that have loans and bills, that will linger around for months or even years, when you can make cash purchases and be debt free, for in my word I gave you instructions to be the lender and not the borrower. Most people make purchases through credit cards and loans.

These things carry a month-to-month balance. This means there are interest charges being added to your monthly statement each month.

But the one thing I knew, sin will prevent you from mending your relationship with God on our own. The Lord said, if I can be jealous, so can you!

Denial

Denial is declaring something to be untrue or a statement that it is not true. When in fact that something is true! It is hard to believe it is me, jealous of debt! Denial is to refuse to admit the truth. We use denial to protect ourselves from the truth.

We cannot allow ourselves to be hurt or be in pain from the problem or issue because we do not want to admit it. Denial is normal to a certain extent. It is also a valid human response to pain. But it should be short-term.

Short-term gives you time to get yourself together, collect your thoughts, words, action, and self-control.

Coming to terms, that you are the one that has the issue or problem. No one wants to admit their jealous of anything, especially when it comes to material things. This is frown upon in the religious arena when people need to talk about it. Confession will cleanse you and make room for deliverance.

Deliverance is healing, and Healing is freedom. You must get yourself organized, body, mind, spirit, and emotions. This will help you handle the truth. And accept the truth about yourself.

*Symptoms of Denial

1. you do not want to talk about the problem or issue

2. You do not even want to think about the problem or the issue

3. you blame everybody else for your problem or issue

4. you say I will take care of it tomorrow and tomorrow never comes

5. you think everyone is against you, you think people do not like you or they are out to get you

6. you love your secret or demon and want to keep it

It is so many symptoms I cannot name them all, but you get the point. If you have any of these symptoms tell yourself, I am ready for a change to take place in my life. This thing is too big for me to manage.

Now it is time for you to get rid of the heavy load. The burden that you have been carrying can be cast away. And your new life can begin with confession. I had to start with repentance.

Repentance

Repentance is sincere regret or remorse. To be truly sorrowful. It is an act of turning away from that thing that held you bowed, captive, caged, confined, enclosed. Stop your practices or deeds so that you can no longer be taken hostage.

Now, you are in a place of humbling yourself. The most powerful and effective place is at the feet of God. A prayer of repentance will help you turn away from your old ways of doing things.

Dear Heavenly Father I come to you sorrowful and humble as I know how. I have full knowledge of my sin and I am ready to repent. Lord, please forgive me for I have sinned against you. Purify me, wash me oh Lord and cleanse me from all unrighteousness. I want to leave this old life behind me and start a new life with you Jesus. Please forgive me for my sins. I am ready to exchange from my carnal mind to having the mind of Christ, from vital to virtue, from darkness to light, from sick to healed, from bondage to freedom, from debt to debt free, from misunderstanding to understanding, from evil to good. Today I will walk in your way and not mine. Amen.

Releasing your Fears

I was ready to be set free. Allow yourself to escape from confinement. There is a process of releasing or being released. I must let somethings go that have me imprisoned.

I was trying to keep up with the Jones's, knowing I did not have the income to do so. Trying to fit into groups that did not even like me, but I wanted social status so that I could get the invite to all the social gatherings I wanted to attend.

Gossiping about those living beneath their means! Those are the people you should be learning from, instead of gossiping about them. Fear is anything that is an unpleasant, often strong emotion caused by the belief that someone or something is a threat.

In the religious setting it means fake evidence appearing real. That is so true. We live our life off lies we believe. Stop hiding behind fear. It is a type of jealousy. Release it and be free.

Deliverance

Deliverance is a state of being delivered from something, it is being rescued or set apart. A feeling of being freed or getting free physically, spiritually, emotionally, and financially. It is a feeling like a ton of bricks are being lifted off you, you feel lighter. As if you are walking on a cloud.

I felt like I was rescued from corruption and bondage. And was set in a place of peace and a joy that you cannot explain. Fear (jealousy) held me hostage for years. I am no longer plagued by the jealousy of debt! I can talk about it. I can face it and deal with it truthfully.

I am no longer lying to myself, about myself, on myself or anyone else. I am in a place now where I can help others. There is nothing better than finding your truth.

That thing that had me bound is now my anointing

God said owe no man nothing but to love him. Now when I see beautiful cars, homes, shoes, and clothes that I would like to have. I see it as debt if I cannot afford to pay cash for it. Debt is like carrying around a ball and chain.

Your debtors have the key, and you cannot get the key until your debt is paid. Debt had me feeling like Rapunzel in the fairytale, locked in the tower with alopecia and unable to carry a tune in a bucket. I will never be jealous of debt again.

If you owe the bank for that fine car you are driving. You are in debt. My motto for debt is I ain't jealous of debt! If you owe that credit card for the tennis bracelet, you are in debt and I ain't jealous of debt! If you owe for that trip to Hawaii with the beautiful pictures, You're in debt and I ain't jealous of debt! I have a new outlook on debt. I ain't jealous of it! I will live a stress-free positive life because I deserve it.

I will encourage others to join in with living financially free!

Poem

This debt dilemma only came to pass,
don't pitch no tent, it won't last, It
may be painful, and it won't be quick,
Just keep your eyes open for the next
debt dilemma trick, Don't be foolish
or naïve, while paying off debts just
believe, You may shed a tear, so
don't despair, God truly care, and
He'll be right there

P.S

When you are trying to get your life or finances in order, trials and tribulations will come so start preparing for the rain because it is going to rain!

www.ingramcontent.com/pod-product-compliance
Lightning Source LLC
LaVergne TN
LVHW052103160826
845678LV00015B/3324

* 9 7 8 0 5 7 8 2 7 1 5 3 8 *